I0760022

p

r

e

c

e

d

e

n

c

e

precedence

pujita verma

BRICK BOOKS
Prince Edward County, Ontario

Library and Archives Canada Cataloguing in Publication
Title: Precedence / Pujita Verma.
Names: Verma, Pujita, author.
Identifiers: Canadiana (print) 20250296268 | Canadiana (ebook) 20250299356 | ISBN 9781771316644 (softcover) | ISBN 9781771316668 (PDF) | ISBN 9781771316651 (EPUB)
Subjects: LCGFT: Poetry.
Classification: LCC PS8643.E738 P74 2026 | DDC C811/.6–dc23

We gratefully acknowledge the Canada Council for the Arts, the Government of Canada through the Canada Book Fund, the Ontario Arts Council, and the Government of Ontario for their support of our publishing program.

Canadä

Canada Council for the Arts   Conseil des Arts du Canada

Edited by Sonnet L'Abbé.
Author photo by Katerina Green.
The book is set in Richmond Text.
Design by Natalie Olsen.

www.brickbooks.ca

Though much of the work of Brick Books takes place on the ancestral lands of the Anishinaabeg, Haudenosaunee, Huron-Wendat, and Mississaugas of the Credit peoples, our editors, authors, and readers from many backgrounds are situated from coast to coast to coast in Canada on the traditional and unceded territories of over six hundred nations who have cared for Turtle Island from time immemorial. While living and working on these lands, we are committed to hearing and returning the rightful imaginative space to the poetries, songs, and stories that have been untold, under-told, wrongly told, and suppressed through colonization.

contents

i

ii

iii

iv

v

vi

i

precedence

noun

/ˈpre-sə-dən(t)s/

: the fact of coming or
occurring earlier in time :

what knowledge haunts each body—
what history, what phantom ache?

NATASHA TRETHEWEY, FROM "MIRACLE OF THE BLACK LEG"

Abecedarian on the Kinds of Distance I Know

apologies
bodies strung into fibre optics
couch cushions & everything between them
dialects you can't learn on Duolingo
elevator ride to my love's apartment
flip phones
glass, shattering at the touch
headboard & wall & everything between
if there is a word for *almost* lonely, I am
just calling to say I miss you
kaleidoscopes
light that fractures
mirror
neurons
#OliveTheory
places you're unwelcome
quiet waiting rooms
recollections
self-preserving stack of mail
Times New Roman of the subpoena
unfinished crescent moons
vectors in space
white flag of a father's laughter
Xmas presents in transit
your left hand
Zoom funerals

Rentrer (v)

in French, there's a word for
coming home. it looks a lot like
re-enter or *renter* and I'm becoming
versed in all of it. when I speak,
it rinses cleaner than cold water
kissing a steel cup. not this Hindi
slowly brought to a simmer in
the markets of New Delhi where
I'm told to hold my tongue. I can't
reconcile with the *mirchi*, distant
summers spread on a dining table
of a childhood's endless leftovers
my mother never taught me to cook
no, I didn't ask her to. or I didn't listen
to recipes that form inheritance, the *masala*
dabba—an exception of time,
each spice spilling over
into the next container

when people asked where I came from,
            I couldn't tell
            I haven't been to my birth country
in a decade. I promised I'd go and visit
and still plan to. sometimes, I trace
the orientation of Google Maps
its unmarked villages, dirt roads
and untranslatable नई दिल्ली dirt roads
what cartographers leave out I'll see
from behind a kitchen counter | a border
I didn't ask my mother the questions
because she stirs as if stroking a cheek
of course, I've heard I can't feel loss
I haven't touched. a place will be set
for me here. I know there is no hunger
if you are still offered something to eat

Wildfire Waking

I was over 3,000 sunsets old / in the back seat of our family minivan / the shade of open
desert for miles / stretches of land / green abbreviations / we are returning from one of those
cross-California road trips / measuring time by intervals between each / road / sign / lines on
lines / yet nothing to say / we don't make it home to Mountain House / in time / we become
the tourniquet of Interstate 205 / smoke dressing a forest's grieving skyline / like you'd wrap
a wound / black clouds inching over a memory / now / after settling somewhere off Ontario's
407 / we are on the futon watching the news in silence / this is how we swallow headlines / fire
season year-long in California / state where my childhood is synonymous with erosion / now
watch frozen freeways from Fort McMurray fires / forced evacuations in BC / Ottawa in orange /
Toronto's air quality the latest newscast disaster / canopy of this city out of focus / my friends on
Draper Lake close all the windows / don't we all breathe in parallel times? / in Canada wildfires
spread coast to coast / unforgiving open arms relentless   in their reach
and isn't this / just another kind of danger / that demands leaving home / without any end in sight

Slide-Jaw

I kept this one secret from my mother
deliberately, the intended intonation

of loose details grinding louder
than a sliding jaw, spaces left

by a tooth pushing itself away
to the edge of three years in silence

I knew that when I'd finally tell her,
the drawing room would overcrowd

at once, that tongue-in-cheek dissolving
in the acknowledgement

that my little sister is growing

we'd do this to keep her safe, yes,
but it isn't like my mother needed

another reason to leave him
so how was I supposed to name

something so unspeakable
if it couldn't also be a diagnosis,

if I couldn't tell her how to cure it
except ask her to carry three children

into the marrow
of a sharpened night

what the conviction fails to capture
my mother will recite in her testimony

anything I cannot keep together,
she always finds a way to hold

Fish Is the Water's Queen

machli jal ki rani hai [the queen of the water is fish]

all I have of my mother tongue
is a saltwater ocean
an iridescent glossary
for unquenchable thirst

jeevan us ka pani hai [and water is her life]

If we are defined by what we can tolerate:
my lungs' lexicon only listens
I cannot stomach spicy food,
shellfish flushes my skin into sun corals

haath lagao gey, dar jaye gi [if you touch her, she will get frightened]

the aunties gather for their gossip,
sharks circling my elementary
diction. a feasting that keeps
this language a fragmented practice

bahar nikaalo gey, mar jaye gi [if you remove her, she will die]

I am out of my depth in speech
but not sentiment. I have gills
proficient at pulling oxygen from Hindi,
drowning my voice when I open my mouth

ii

unprecedented

adjective

/ˌən-ˈpre-sə-ˌden-təd/

: never done or known before :

They were things for which it was impossible to prepare but which one spent a lifetime looking back at, trying to accept, interpret, comprehend.

JHUMPA LAHIRI, FROM *THE NAMESAKE*

Lessons on Transmigration

My father is teaching about reincarnation
over a table of holy oak. He calls the soul *atman* and each life,

a cycle of *samsara*. I pass the aloo gobi,
watching the dish migrate above this lifeless tree.

One day, I'll understand we're a lot like each other:
We both left home for a better life

sanded and smoothed in our sequencing.
My father tells us death is simply transition.

That my *atman* can be reborn
and reborn and reborn

and if I rack up enough bad karma,
I'll return to the world

an inanimate object.
I can't recall if there was a god keeping score

for my soul's metempsychosis,
just that the one night in my bed

he was there, I had to lay so still,
I didn't know if I had died

and woken up inanimate.
My body, placed in a blanket

paralysis that time could not ease
the movement for.

We have not spoken in six years
though I want to tell him:

When you are gone,

I will not know in which discount furniture store
I might find you ossified within.

Antyesti

Hindu funeral rites for the dead, when a body is cremated and the ashes are dispersed in the Ganga, where it is customary to bathe an infant as a rite of passage

I do not pretend to be housing pearls
under skin of dirt,
no seeds to meet water
under layers of farmland

on this side of the Atlantic
protest is 7 o'clock news:
white noise to douse
conversation

Nani's English never takes flight
before our hands press together again
her *hellos* are translated as *goodbyes*
as if a Wi-Fi's hesitation

could hang the call. as if she is a match
that will light her daughter's
passage back,
ghar aa jao (come home)

there, all the women put themselves on mute
to hear my poems. see
eyes spill. fill Ganga's streams
like ash in macrocosm

even if they cannot disperse
a word–
or my mother tongue
is stifled by their sacrifices

my eloquence is tribute. this lineage,
burdened with drowning
women. from the 1,500-mile stretch
between Northern India

and the Bay of Bengal. our holiest river
is swollen with bodies
girls they could not marry
could not carry their elements

back to origins. I will tell you a story
in which they are at rest,
now carried by remnant
ashes and river-rocked to sleep

I have tasted their soot
and struggle. we were birthed
from universal womb,
have bathed together

with each rite of *samsara,*
(my mother once brought
me to bathe in the riverbeds,
long before I could walk)

to the collective, unbecoming act
of cleansing from his fingerprints
how pure we are,
and no one is looking

believe me. there is nothing beautiful to make
of the burning,
of wearing white
to the pyre,

of an aisle unrolled by flame, of a vow
afloat a bitten tongue, of a body
reclaimed entirely in backstroke
I will swim home

in any language I can cauterize
aap ki kahaani / kaee kaanon tak / jaye gi
(your story will reach many ears)
until we meet again

Tetris Trucks

one thing about leaving home:
it isn't always planned, can just be
a confession to your mother

on the bedroom floor, detour to the
police station. being told to stay
away from home & turn off
your locations. enter: the spring

of geographic exile,   one carry-on
to carry on   the house hunt.   recall:
cigarette burns   on motel sheets,
shut-eye   at Greyhound Station
kindness of friends who let you   stay,
miss the emergency   geared-to-income
application.   reasons to deny a lease:
three kids, inflating trepidation

then summer,   a chance to stay
somewhere together.   unaffordable
housing   rooted by light   seeping in
a 2-foot basement window: just enough   to see
beneath dirt. stems reaching   for sky
we still needed to go back   for all our stuff,
cruiser at curb   for police-supervised visit
Tetris trucks on moving day, loading   ramp:
a ticking clock,   race against a rushing night

so many things   were left   behind
(rollerblades, trophy case, albums worn by time)
        they must sit somewhere now, right?
                think of: family
histories dispersed   on thrift store shelving,
relics of a storage facility   landfills surfacing
allegories.   now make most   of the space
you have.   hang up pre-loved   frames

& 7 cuckoo clocks
& tall glass jars
& square mirrors
& sea glass slivers
& brass silverware
& unbound albums
& Dollarama decor
& tuck
& stack
& stick
just watch
you'll
fill every
last inch
of the space

Raccoon in Basement Window

lock eyes at 2 a.m., matching dark circles
small hands inching to press cold glass
subject: two creatures peeking through portals
keeping them enclosed, searching
for own coveted shelters. burrowing
for winter and all seasons

I watch the racoons
the way I watch the world
when I can't sleep:
| through a screen |
or behind bolted door. raccoon & I coexist
though I'm not sure which one of us is witness
we understand our places
why we choose them
the need to settle, burrow, watch, hope;
I also hope we won't be staying here for long

when visiting home
I sleep on sofa bed, listen for small
steps. we rubber-band our trash bins but see
tiny footprints trailing snow
I try not to afford myself luxury
of leaving a trail

iii

precedent

noun

/ˈpre-sə-dənt/

: a legal decision or form of proceeding serving as an authoritative rule or pattern in future similar or analogous cases :

Tell all the Truth but tell it slant –

EMILY DICKINSON

Crown Attorney Affirmations
punctuate time and all its verdicts:

you should feel very lucky
that you've come this far.

most cases will never see
the inside of a courtroom,
a comma splice
of collective amnesia
disentangling for scribbling strangers.

the reports are indicative
no defence lawyer
will produce a discography
of your callouses, your
articulation is an asterisk
of the witness stand.

watch walls come falling
at your feet, it takes
as much courage as these proceedings
take time. think

of your little sister,
how she might get to grow up
outside the margins,

think
of the precedent
you are setting,

everyone who may get to stand
in line
beside you.

(UN)OFFICIAL TRANSCRIPT

Court Filing No: TBD

If all testimony fractures memory,
to recall is to rewrite sensory.

Incessant day stuck on repeat;
broken record played between the teeth.

A cue's a queue in disguise–
scripts dictate these stories.

If to stand trial is to test performance
then watch the record

record stutter.
Semantics strangle

this opposition:
Bona fide v. Contrived

but don't all truths
brew-into-each-other?

One morning gathers
years on standby,

jumping
rope

on
jargon.

Synapses short-circuit
waiting on answer–

somewhere, a swinging door
rocks on and on.

The Purpose of Subsection 7 (4.1)

of the *Criminal Code*
R.S.C., 1985, c. C-46

as interpreted by the trial judge:

"the deterrence of Canadian citizens and permanent residents from engaging in what, by Canadian standards, is seen as exploitive sexual activity of children while abroad"

as suggested by the Crown:

"in light of what were perceived
as failures of or limitations on
the international community in dealing with this issue"

as asserted by defence:

"infringes. . .liberty interests
in a way that is contrary to the principles of
fundamental justice in that it is overbroad"

as responded to by me (the constitutional challenge):

I should be thankful: I'm a citizen of a country
where the courts will convict for me. I wrestle
irony of this prosecution, if years before,

I'd been *out of jurisdiction.*
except the challenge of location
can't escape me. if I am stranger

to displacement, then all places
can erase me. I traced lineage
like an oath. or a precedence

for promise. held passport envy
close, foreign headlines
as a homage. think of the children

outside the law, line drawn
between here | abroad.
if the question of selection

predetermines disposition:
when my father filed our papers,
he left out my mother's application.

our nationalities span on
fault lines, foreshadowed
fractured family. I wore

her former favourite blouse
to my citizenship
ceremony.

Defence Attorney Asks

if it could've been a dream:

I know I know I didn't say anything
for years   but I know
it happened   when it did,
I remember the day   after,
silent drive to last art class
of summer camp,   hours of sketching

bodiless   shapes. actually I remember
that long night   too, its enduring dawn,
    Dubai sun still rising
like   collateral   for this skin.
I remember the nonstop flight to Toronto,
    thinking about the taxonomy

of   ink,   being fifteen,
then the   weeks   after
the   months   within,
  becoming an accountant
of my own   upbringing, as
if there were   early signs
of stain, dye, or sublimation.

yes I'm aware I was silent
for so long,   I   also kept
inventory of the days I thought
        nothing of it
but isn't that the dangerous thing
about a burning memory:

it will singe everything it reaches.
        I know,
        I forgot   until forgetting
made   my ignorance
        an endless   desert,
bleaching everything along with it.

as interpreted by the trial judge:

“the complainant’s actions   between the alleged
            and when she went to police were consistent
            young girl who had been assaulted
‘not prepared to report to others or confront the perpetrator,
given his role in her life’”

The Conviction but [Redacted]

Code of
Section *Interference*

who, for a purpose, touches, directly or indirectly,
the body an object,
under the age

(a) is indictable and is
a term of minimum

an offence
liable more than
imprisonment

Redacted [Conviction]

Section

person who,
part
s of

guilt liable

imprisonment

is
not
punishment

~~The Conviction but~~ Rewritten

of Interference

a term for who?
every person with a body part
is not object
or imprisonment

the summary of a body
is more than indictable,
more than any touches of offence

a person of conviction
is liable to a purpose,
for a term of day
to days–years
and
years

The Publication Ban:

(a)
is a right to protect you. or encourage you to come forward. granted at your request. or placed upon you if you are/were a child. on sensitive cases. or against your consent?

(b)
sparks continued confusion about *whose* identity is covered by the ban. contradicting consistency of this legal practice varying in application.

(c)
restricts your ability to transmit/broadcast/publish your experience. max fine of $5,000 and/or two years less a day of jail time. plus a victim surcharge.

(d)
sanctions victim's non-compliance, *can be more severe than your offender's sentence* (max sentence for some charges on summary conviction is 18 months).

(e)
will make protection and isolation apposite. no one really understands the ban, especially you. be careful. you can't trust your intuition, tell anyone of your proximity to the crime.

(f)
can be lifted. can be denied to be lifted? can allow case on why it shouldn't be lifted? can make your life a lyrical selection; your story synonymous with its silence.

Zoom Courtroom in Three Acts

I.

Papa—I never wanted to sentence you
only ask if you were proud of me
the jury is still out.

I did not want you to think of me
as a daughter with a question mark

asking more than what she deserved.
we are on two sides of the virtual trial:
the complainant

|

the accused
a liquid-crystal display
dividing two generations

II.

of injustices. I took the Officer's advice
testified to a bright yellow Post-it note
        covering your face,
not sure if your eyeline would meet mine

in an ellipses
        or maybe
                an apology.

III.

now, I find out about the new family
          through the court order,
I know they know, but do they know

how my mind's fabric
is chiffon, letting light slip
through its transparencies.

they must have only seen you:
          a father in recovery.
the kind I would press my forehead

against the glass window
and wait for,
hoping to find
          on his way home.

Double Criminality

in lecture, I learn how justice can be
a culturally-bound concept. just as moral

relativism confines what is right or wrong,
our ideas of what is *deserved*

can be territorially tested. I needed to know
everything about double criminality. how the defence

articulated extra-jurisdiction. now legal language
permeates all spheres of my life:

a lexicon by which to interpret
the unspeakable. there is a point where my settle

becomes surrender. and how much easier
it was to turn up on my side of the courtroom

speak truth without regard to outcome.
I read my impact statement

at the sentencing, my first in-person appearance
since lockdowns lifted.

            he did not plead guilty.
so his incarceration means nothing

except to the state. the case was heard
at Ontario's appeals court; so due process

is reinforced when the state retraces its steps.
these days I feel I'm free to step outside the house

without chin over shoulder, watching my back.
to me, justice is a careless bar crawl on

Richmond Row. a live story I post to IG
(with my location tag) or writing typewriter poetry

for strangers at festivals. justice is life revelling
in normalcy. existence without the backdrop of traceable fear

without the backdrop of intangible grief. which is always coded
by guilt. my mind fails me because I want to believe

in the good of people, but memory destroys this dichotomy:
it demands to be recollected in disunion. and justice too

can be just as disjointed.
the sentence will end, as I will

once again return to closed spaces.

iv

p r e v a l e n c e

noun

/ˈpre-və-lən(t)s/

: the fact that something is very common or happens often :

neighbours silent as a blown fuse.
houses in a blank-eyed row.

JODY CHAN, FROM "CPTSD: EMOTIONAL FLASHBACK"

2nd Session, 35th Parliament,
45-46 Elizabeth II, 1996-97

The House of Commons of Canada

BILL C-27

An Act to amend the Criminal Code (child prostitution, child sex tourism, criminal harassment and female genital mutilation)

The Unreported

statistics will tell you
everything you need to know
nothing you'd want to

prevalence of abuse is not anomaly
instead anticipated
most likely someone you may know

nicknames for non-strangers
we give to define proximity
to those we can trust

what about distrust of world
after growing up in parentheses
what it takes to not come forward

I used to keep an archive
hidden photo gallery & voice memos
in case burden of proof came to knock

but after cops   CPS visits
echo chamber of certainty
suspended by not coming forward

the duty to report distorts
when it's your fingers over keypad
ready to dial

but not
ready to make the call

(f)
the need to be important, for the self to take priority. over anonymity,
acronym, abbreviation. to reverse search court file #

(e)
scale its precedent against protection
end up reading case after case after self-identifying

(d)
as a #. to disrupt silence again after own inarticulate years
redacting & redacting until I've rendered myself meaningless

(c)
my circular language has an origin: courtroom defines me
victim | complainant | daughter | sometimes as survivor

(b)
most days I don't want to be subject to interpretation

(a)
the more I escape what defines me, everything blooms in its exception
like centripetal force, I revolve around blank spaces

On Lifting ~~the Publication Ban~~

WE BUY GOLD

there is a process of melting   what you know   removing its impurities
forgive ancestral inheritance   in exchange   for rewritten precedent:
selling ~~grandmother's~~ Nani's gold at a pawn shop   to keep lights on
leaving a legacy of women who could not leave.   my mother not named
in the family will, a way birthright can be selective   of gender. on another

continent, Nani collected precious metals   in her closet's labyrinth
called this exit strategy for her daughter: an intergenerational justice. watch
whole wars wage for a commodity worth more   than its weight in memory
think   *jhumkis, bangles, maang tikka–*   a lineage
of wedding adornments passed down in ceremony.   it takes three years

before I locate lexicon, tell my mother. she believes me.   we leave
customs of culture & a women's candidacy; those teach us fear & retribution
as resistant to corrosion. I'm shopping   markets of Chandni Chowk
while Nani drifts   in the CCU   after waiting decade to re-meet
grandchild   passing time   until visiting window

opens briefly–   threads of my new *lehengas* unravelling.   I'd learned Hindi
through an app for months   before making trip to Delhi,   her village
dialect   I still couldn't dissect   without intermediary.   all I'd know of her
is an untranslation of proximity.   how she'd been engaged at eight
(age, another theory of relativity). last time I'd see her & I couldn't articulate

goodbye,   cycles of reincarnation eclipsing gratitude.   at her wake,
neighbours tell me how they'd watched her hold me,   a baby on the balcony
basking in   the sunlight's glory.   there is a process of melting
what you are told about purity.   remember, even love can be an economy
of scale. like golden hope, when abundant, will tip everything in your favour

Kal

I miss you more than I remember you

OCEAN VUONG, FROM *ON EARTH WE'RE BRIEFLY GORGEOUS*

the Hindi word
for yesterday
is same as its word for tomorrow
कल : both reminiscence
& promise. all I have of you
is enough to carry (you) onwards
looking forward to endless
yesterdays with you

Excerpts from a ~~VICTIM IMPACT STATEMENT~~ Breakup

We grow up
freely.
recognize
fault.
not
hurt I grew up too fast.
afraid
vivid
night
s appear
resilient
hate touch
have to re-learn love
distanced me
distanced
me

envied friends able to experience
willing l y.
felt alone for years
unpacking
shame
I did not ask for. I want safe
body
cemented
exhausted. move forward
truth spoke
I
am okay I get up
will
struggle to sleep
will always be part of me
lost
t o
someone I once loved

V

prescribe

verb

/pri-ˈskrīb/

: to order treatment for :
alternatively
: to lay down a rule :

do you recall,
for an instant, the narrow things widening?

DOYALI ISLAM, FROM "IN JOHNSON STRAIT"

Epidemic of Inattention

processing capacity of the conscious mind is measured by units of information
about 50 bits per second / bandwidth of traffic for my
head's ceaseless highways / I'm not sure if I've evolved to process so
many bits at once / my attentional filter, a window left wide
open neurons working overtime to fire away while Zoloft numbs
my hard drive / I've been filling prescriptions below speed limit / yet vivid
streetlights blur together like data descent of doomscroll / nights defined
by "one last reel" before sleep / each pixel replays in REM cycles
I mean, my faith in the algorithm keeps me / / / / content
with self-isolation / sustained focus is cognitive dissonance
when I bear witness to worlds of injustice / without leaving four walls
complicit in closing doors / the way content creators are in crafting clickbait
earth's data is measured in exabytes / my output is everything I scroll past, like
ads headlines notifications non-urgent emails / friends asking how I've been
I haven't been / around / maybe I hurt the ones I love because I know how to
ignore them / overthink each reply / a pressured paralysis / deflecting the time

Tham Luang Cave Rescue

moments my fingers hover over your
unopened messages, things I want to tell you
become my monsoon. I finally saw the film. you
know the one about the trapped soccer team
& the world that swarmed to Tham Luang cave to pull honey
from the heart's wound? that one. true story. I
was making tea when divers first discovered the bodies
I mean the boys
(they were found alive) & I
was licking gold syrup off my fingers
been years since the divers
brought them back (alive, yes, but conscious?
not exactly) & I can't stop thinking about the boys
sticking to higher ground & they
kept climbing further & you
told me how long it took, for the fields to finally forgive
the farmers, for diverting the water. letting them flood. (I wonder if you
know I've been treading water. you are in growing season.) families
were camped in the mouth of the hive & others
split. or dared to step into the stomach
you tell me years ago your father
followed this allegory, as rescue divers
pressed between two walls & found footing
to climb further. I
think necessity paves the way for all
the strength someone
could ever have
there's so much I
want to tell you
& nothing that I
need to. searching for you
might just cave inside of me

everything always ends
with the body

(scars)

i don't know how to write about
the silver scars, which healed
like parallel ridges of Himalayas,
don't define me but have
been used to describe me
self-inflicted, yes, which
misnames origin of harm but is
sediment metamorphic rock
rising each year. i don't
know how to emerge sleeveless
without making statement
be seismic yet self-contained
there's a sacred journey
8.5 million take onto Trikuta
mountain each year; my own
trek begins at the foothill
of old bathroom, after i'd free
mirror from hinges, slide panel
to reveal graphite words i etched

onto orange-peach wall.   yes,
i've drawn borders   on this body
anyone to touch my arms   since
has been tender, sealing tectonic
movement   like glacial kiss,
un-prescribing fault   from line
but i want to be loved   *because*
and not *despite.*   all the years
cross-examining this skin when
i could've been   in my own
corner.   my capacity to cope
does not undermine   capacity
of a touch to erode,   i spoke
the scars
into courtroom   when asked
of this body's   topography,
transcriptors preserving   every
erasure. so perhaps it's all   I can
ever let them be–   testimony

Ode to Aloe Vera

ingredient of hand soap
or shaving cream for the sensitive
& irrational. or reassurance
for a tingling scalp & its overthinker
a halo of floating foam, dissolving at the prospect of water
like a horizon, hoarder of the sun's rays
my vibrant sky—an open flame
cold gel to dress a wound
or myself. on the days love
was not enough, could not pull me
from bed, ease me through the day
Aloe vera: a form of salvation,
something to reduce the inflammation,
lock in the moisture, wrap its limbs
around while I'm healing, growing,
regenerating with thicker skin
a leaf to peel back & place on the lips,
after I'd picked them into a new shade
of the night sky. I wished myself to settle
under my surface. worried myself
to be the only one I was certain I could reach for,
an over-the-counter cure
that will always soften
the burn

vi

proceed

verb

/prō-ˈsēd/

: to move on :

is everything you love foreign
or are you foreign to everything you love?

WARSAN SHIRE, FROM "MIDNIGHT IN THE FOOD AISLE"

Abecedarian on How to Forget Someone

apologize
block them, no
call. wait for
dial tone & say
everything you wish you could
forget about them
ghost their hovering memory
how they touched you
in the absence of daylight,
just enough to
keep you tethered
lie. it meant nothing to you
make a big deal of
numerical anomalies
on the birthday of someone you used to love
photographs will make you
question your
recollection
suspend the disbelief in
therapy, think about when they've let you down
undress for the closest star
vivid hope of extraterrestrial existence
when people ask, shrug. say. . . *we don't talk anymore*
xerox the DMs before you delete them
years & years will pass. you will
zone out when they cross your mind

The Degree of Disorder

(solid)

you've been cautioned of strangers
but hasn't everyone, at the start,

been someone you didn't know?
now they're people you could ring

if you'd just pick up the phone–
the entropy of your empathy:

life's disorders dictating the distances

spaces we keep
between those we keep close

(liquid)

you don't know if there's more distance
between stranger or someone estranged

your whole life, you've tried
to make friends. find *your people*

but you're a shapeshifter
flowing in between states

testing terminal velocity of trust

when it falls. the love you came from
is liquid. flowing in displacement

what relations could be formed
without honest foundations

(gas)

there's balance in dissolution of what you know. a natural chaos
to govern what it means to belong

all the rooms you enter
arrythmic arrivals

friends who could not understand, but they do
sit with you, while you're trying not to

you're learning some things don't merit comprehension
instead you talk about unreliable narrators

& plot holes. concerts that could change your lives,
antigravity of songs that bring you to flight

circular rebirth of time & the times
you show up. cosmic equilibrium restores

you're still trying to place yourself
in this messy universe, the friends are with you through every shift

love is being witness
not thermodynamics

you're shaping them a prayer into the anatomy
of a promise: to take care of themselves

& you will too

Sonnet of Indifference

The opposite of love is not hate, it's indifference

ELIE WIESEL, FROM *U.S. NEWS AND WORLD REPORT*

would you tell me, if you knew of something
more lonely than the staccato of a Sunday?
I caught my steeping tea blushing
in the golden honey of a sun ray
I'm writing lists on lists
without a soul to listen–
could someone stay to coexist,
to watch the trivial glisten?

they're here, I think, in another room
but thawing love is out of touch;
we don't speak without the moon,
could my presence be too much?

for all this solitude, I should be grateful–
the light will spill & always stay so faithful

Somatic Symphony Softness

is new to muscle memory
have you truly heard of love–
did you know it comes so gently?

Our Tinder Story

at Pinery Provincial Park

    you tend an open flame
gas station firewood is
    crackling at us
as if a reminder I haven't seen you
    in any other light. you,
choreographer of the forest's limbs
    careful, contemporary,
always one step
    away
from consumed
    I met you online,
a flash point of modern romance
    with you,
there is no need to retreat
    when the heat
becomes palpable, or when
    carbon embers
sizzle sleeves. all your touch
    is a magnitude short
of placement
    on the Mercalli scale–
Pinery's Oak Savanna
    swaying
as I watch you
    feed kindling
to the coals

before this,
I'd only known of
dissociative touch
the kind of survival
that demands us to watch
our own bodies
from a distance. new love
is an act of self-preservation:
how we are kind
to the memory of what has shaken us
I've become the kind of woman who folds
last month's flyers into newspaper flowers
these are perfect, you tell me,
look how they feed the flame
a firefly frenzy dances for us,
drifting smoke rises higher
than the forest's canopy

Footnotes for the Toronto Sky

before, I didn't think there was such a thing
as too much light. this city blinds its own night
there are supposed to be 4,500 stars visible
from where we stand[1]

we took the last ferry to Centre Island,
for a moment, captured the city's behemoth
as a simple subject of our visual fields, edge to edge,
everything brilliant the bulbs of an eye could hold

on the walk back, we followed a road not illuminated
by any street lamp. talked about how one day,
if an apartment made sense & we could afford the view,
we might become one of the beautiful, flickering windows

---

1 I see only you

One Point of Contact

as we doze off, please,
just one palm
softly on this shoulder, an arm
around your waist, or a toe
traversing the flat sheet's
sweeping meanders, or
mend spaces with one string
tied to your finger
for the nights you crash on the couch,
let me be the memory foam
for all your landings,
tell me which one god
forms the worship
of your midnight
mumbles, I'll rehearse
that prayer until every one-
rous day paves a road
back to you, or
we don't have to hang
up the call now, just one more
minute until we fall
asleep,

Small Sanctuaries

which had always been impenetrably ours, even before this new life
our family made. seconds before sleep snaps. kettle's quivering wake
& subsequent steep. chai warming its holder. running a midday bath
to drown sound with crashing water. whisper-conversations. tapestries hung
over a wall's imperfect holes. I used to keep an archive. now I can't
bring myself to watch it. except to see how far we've come. we're patient
with our unlearnings–that's the best I could've hoped for. I'm finding love
in little rituals. what perseveres after we're tired of persevering
& just want to be. there are certainties, like fortune cookies
we read in a circle. tub of Nivea care we akin to Ganga water. of course,
the rising heat of baths too, but no more surfacing sound to level out
our small sanctuaries expanding into weeks, metres, decibels, years
of exercises in trust fall restoring balance. I have to remind
myself: refuge isn't fleeting escapes but places you can call home
precedent can be rewritten & you never had to do it alone

Glossary

नई दिल्ली	New Delhi
कल/ *kal*	word for both yesterday and tomorrow
aloo gobi	a potato and cauliflower dish
atman	a person's soul
chai	tea
Chandni Chowk	a busy market in the heart of Old Delhi, known for spices, jewellery, bridal wear, vivid saris, and more
Ganga	the Ganges River
jhumkis, maang tikka	South Asian jewellery
lehenga	a long skirt often elaborately embroidered with beads, mirrors, or other ornaments
masala dabba	stainless steel or brass container for storing spices
mirchi	hot, as well as the word for chili pepper
samsara	repeated cycles of death and rebirth
Trikuta	three-peaked mountain, and sacred pilgrimage site in Jammu and Kashmir

Notes

Precedence quotes from the following sources:

Doyali Islam, *heft* (McClelland & Stewart, 2019)
Elie Wiesel, *U.S. News and World Report* (27 October 1986)
Emily Dickinson, *Poems: Second Series* (Roberts Brothers, 1891)
Jhumpa Lahiri, *The Namesake* (Mariner Books Classics, 2019)
Jody Chan, *impact statement* (Brick Books, 2024)
Natasha Trethewey, *Thrall* (Ecco, 2015)
Ocean Vuong, *On Earth We're Briefly Gorgeous* (Penguin Press, 2019)
Warsan Shire, *Bless the Daughter Raised by a Voice in Her Head* (Random House Trade Paperbacks, 2022)

All pronunciation keys across chapter title pages were sourced from *Merriam-Webster*. The definitions for the words across chapter title pages come from the following sources:

"precedence" from Part I is from *Merriam-Webster*
"unprecedented" from Part II is adapted from the *Oxford English Dictionary*
"precedent" from Part III is from *Collins*
"prevalence" from Part IV is from *Cambridge Dictionary*
"prescribe" from Part V is from *Cambridge Dictionary* and *Merriam-Webster*
"proceed" from Part VI is adapted from *Collins*

"Epidemic of Inattention" references the fact that the processing capacity of our conscious mind can be measured at 50 bits per second. Though this is a widely cited statistic, some sources indicate it could be as low as 10 bits per second.

"(scars)" references 8.5 million pilgrims making the sacred journey to Trikuta each year. This was reported in 2018 by the Vaishno Devi shrine.

"Footnotes for the Toronto Sky" references 4,500 stars visible in the night sky. This is a possible estimate calculated by apparent magnitude from our hemisphere and based on nearly impossible and perfect viewing conditions.

Publications

"Abecedarian on the Kinds of Distance I Know" appeared in the League of Canadian Poets' *Poetry Pause.*

"Antyesti" first appeared in the *Maza Anthology* and again in the *Winged Penny Review.*

"Fish Is the Water's Queen" appeared in *FreeFall Magazine.*

"Footnotes for the Toronto Sky" was featured across the Toronto Transit Commission network as part of the inaugural Poems in Passage season.

"One Point of Contact" and "Abecedarian on How to Forget Someone" appeared in *Stones Beneath the Surface Poetry Anthology*, published by Black Mallard Poetry.

"Tham Luang Cave Rescue" won the 2023 League of Canadian Poets Broadsheet Contest. It follows the story of an extraordinary 2018 cave rescue in Thailand.

"(UN)OFFICIAL TRANSCRIPT," "Wildfire Waking," and an earlier version of "Rentrer (v)" appeared in the Eden Mills Writers Festival *emerge* chapbook, published by Publication Studio Guelph.

"WE BUY GOLD" won the 2024 Arts and Letters Club of Toronto Foundation Poetry Award.

Acknowledgements

Deepest Gratitude:

To my mother, who taught love and resilience as synonymous acts. My Nani and the legacy of fierce women who paved the way. My brother and sister who brave each chapter with me.

To you, for listening. If you feel seen in these poems–know I am standing in line beside you.

To funding from the Ontario Arts Council. To the invaluable support from Diaspora Dialogues and the Banff Centre for Arts and Creativity.

To my mentor Doyali Islam, for teaching me empathetic integrity and the economy of language. To Sharanpal Ruprai for your care, laughter, and encouragement from the start of this collection.

To the incredible Brick Books team. To my editor Sonnet L'Abbé for inviting me to explore each word and poem in a new light. Manahil Bandukwala for your mentorship and inspiration. Alayna Munce for believing in this manuscript. Natalie Olsen for the incisive cover design.

To Maria Thorburn, Alberts Vitols, and Alastair Thorburn-Vitols, for being there. From my early poetry journey to opening your home and sharing the purpose of art in this world.

To my poetry professors, David Barrick, Kateri Lanthier, and Kathryn Mockler. My friends at Antler River Poetry. Kathryn Garland from the City of Mississauga.

To inspiring conversations and people who have held space for me over the years: Qurat, Liv, Alyssa, Emi, Amandeep, Zeest,

Misha, Devi, Aleks, Roméo, Srishti, Simran, Manroop, Linda, Leon, Katie, Seema, + Shantanu.

To Karen Bellehuemer and everyone from the Officers, Victim/Witness Assistance Program, to the Crown, whose dedication reshapes my perspectives on justice.

To my friends at War Child.

To Sonja, Richard, and Katerina Green, for all your love and this beautiful home.

To my partner in everything, Christopher Green, for the courage to write from the heart.

Pujita Verma is a poet and illustrator currently living in London, Ontario. Her work has appeared across the Toronto Transit Commission Network and on CBC's *The National*. She has won awards from the League of Canadian Poets, the Toronto Arts & Letters Club Foundation, and the Eden Mills Writer's Festival, and was runner-up for the Janice Colbert Poetry Award. Pujita was Mississauga's Youth Poet Laureate from 2018–2020, and she studied Political Science at Western University. As an active member of London's literary scene, Pujita is currently serving on the committee for Antler River Poetry.

Printed by Imprimerie Gauvin
Gatineau, Québec